IF I COULD DRIVE A
TONKA TRUCK!

IF I COULD DRIVE A
TONKA TRUCK!

If I Could Drive a **BULLDOZER!**

If I Could Drive a **DUMP TRUCK!**

If I Could Drive a **FIRE TRUCK!**

If I Could Drive a **LOADER!**

If I Could Drive a **TOW TRUCK!**

SCHOLASTIC I
New York   Toronto   London
Mexico City   New Delhi   Ho

If I Could Drive a BULLDOZER!, ISBN 0-439-34175-2, Copyright © 2002 Hasbro, Inc.

If I Could Drive a DUMP TRUCK!, ISBN 0-439-31814-9, Copyright © 2001 Hasbro, Inc.

If I Could Drive a FIRE TRUCK!, ISBN 0-439-31815-7, Copyright © 2001 Hasbro, Inc.

If I Could Drive a LOADER!, ISBN 0-439-31816-5, Copyright © 2001 Hasbro, Inc.

If I Could Drive a TOW TRUCK!, ISBN 0-439-36587-2, Copyright © 2002 Hasbro, Inc.
Interior design by Bethany Dixon.

TONKA® is a registered trademark of Hasbro, Inc. Used with permission.

12 11 10 9 8 7 6 5 4 3 2 1   5 6 7 8 9 10/0

Printed in the U.S.A.   24

This edition created exclusively for Barnes & Noble, Inc.

2005 Barnes & Noble Books

ISBN 0-7607-9543-6

First compilation printing, May 2005

CONTENTS

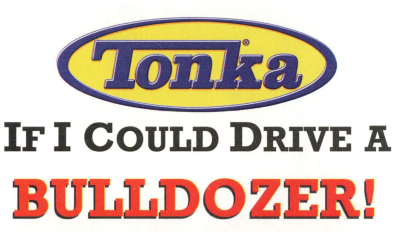

Tonka

If I Could Drive a
BULLDOZER!

by Michael Teitelbaum
Illustrated by Uldis Klavins

My name is Matt, and I really love playing with trucks.

My favorite truck is the bulldozer.

I play with my toy bulldozer in the backyard, pushing dirt and rocks around.

Sometimes I pretend that my bulldozer is knocking down an old building to make room for a new one.

What if *I* could drive a bulldozer?

A bulldozer can weigh as much as ten tons! It is like a tank with a large steel blade on the front. A bulldozer doesn't have wheels. It rolls on special crawler treads.

The treads make it easy for the bulldozer to roll over rough ground. They also help hold up the bulldozer's heavy weight. That way, the weight is spread over a big area, so the bulldozer doesn't sink into the mud.

My bulldozer's sharp blade stays close to the ground, cutting through even the hardest soil.

The blade can be raised, lowered, or even tilted to reach just the right angle.

Because of its crawler treads, a bulldozer can't ride on the road like other trucks. I drive my bulldozer onto the back of a big truck called a tractor trailer. Then the tractor trailer drives along paved roads, carrying the bulldozer. That's how I get my bulldozer to the job site.

At the job site, I drive my bulldozer down the tractor trailer's ramp. Now it's ready to work.

Usually, my bulldozer is the first truck at the site. It prepares the site so that other trucks can do their jobs.

Today I am helping a farmer by knocking down his old barn. Then I'll help prepare the site for a new barn to be built.

The old barn was starting to fall down on its own, and it was too dangerous to use anymore. Working carefully, my bulldozer helps to push down the rest of the crumbling building.

Then I push the broken pieces of the barn away to make room for the new one.

Finally, I use the bottom of the bulldozer's blade to push the dirt and smooth out the ground.
Now the new barn can be built!

The bulldozer's work is done now.
Some other trucks arrive. Here comes a loader to scoop, a backhoe to dig, and a dump truck to carry away the wood from the old barn.

And that's what I would do if I could drive a bulldozer!

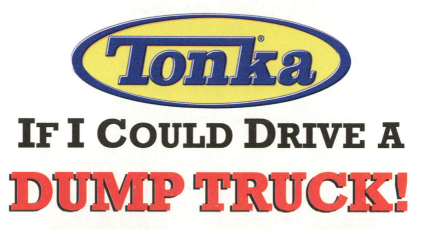

IF I COULD DRIVE A

DUMP TRUCK!

by Michael Teitelbaum
Illustrated by Uldis Klavins

My name is Ben.
This is my toy dump truck. I like to pretend that my sandbox is a big construction site.

What if *I* could drive a dump truck?

The back part of my dump truck is called the bed. The stuff that I'm carrying goes there.

My dump truck can carry gravel, sand, rocks, or dirt. A covering keeps the load from falling out while I travel.

The great thing about my dump truck is that I can unload it without help from anyone else!

I press a lever in the cab. Then the bed lifts up and the gravel pours out.

My dump truck and I help at the site of a new building. Sometimes big loads of dirt need to be moved from one part of a construction site to another.

Another truck, called a loader, fills my dump truck with dirt.

Next, my dump truck and I help landscapers make a beautiful garden. First my dump truck carries in a load of topsoil.

Then I dump a load of wood mulch. The mulch is made from shredded branches that have been trimmed from trees. It protects the topsoil.

Finally, my dump truck dumps a load of large stepping stones. The landscapers will use these stones to create a path through the garden.

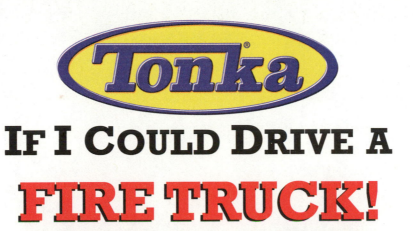

IF I COULD DRIVE A

FIRE TRUCK!

by Michael Teitelbaum

Illustrated by Uldis Klavins and Jeff Walker

My name is Susan.
Today, I'm going to visit Grandma with my mom and dad.
It's a long drive, but I've got my favorite fire truck to play with.

WHEE-OOH! WHEE-OOH! WHEE-OOH!
A real fire truck races past us on its way to an emergency.
My dad moves our car out of the way and slows down.
Wow, look at that fire truck go!
What if *I* could drive a fire truck?

I would start my day in the fire station with all the other firefighters.

CLANG! CLANG! CLANG! CLANG! CLANG!

The alarm sounds. There's a fire in a house on Chestnut Street.

Everyone springs into action. Down the pole I slide!

We race to our ladder truck. The ladder can go up to reach high windows. Our truck also carries hoses for water and axes and saws for getting into burning buildings.

Some of the firefighters stand on the truck's back bumper. They hold onto handles so they don't fall off. I drive.

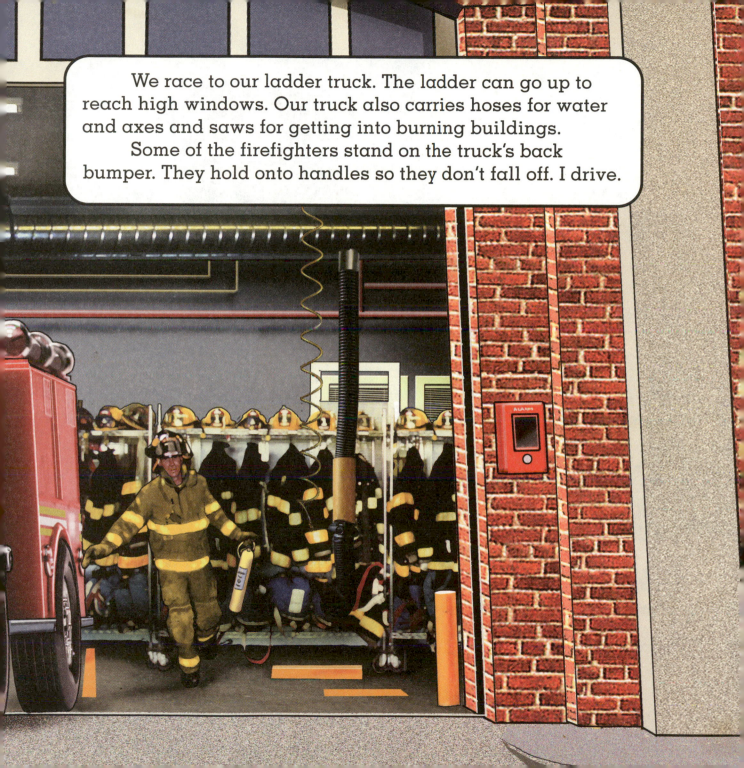

I speed through the streets with my siren screaming. *WHEE-OOH! WHEE-OOH! WHEE-OOH!*
The other cars get out of my way. They know I'm racing to fight a fire, and every second counts!

In a few minutes, we arrive at the fire. The top floor of a house is burning. Flames and smoke pour from the windows. The family who lives there has gotten out safely. Now it's up to us to save their home.

A police car screeches to a halt. The fire chief's truck is right behind it. Police officers keep the crowd safely away from the fire. The fire chief directs the firefighters as we battle the blaze.

Then an ambulance shows up to help any people who may be hurt.

I attach one end of my hose to the fire hydrant. Once the hydrant is opened, water will rush through the hose.

Next, we raise our tall ladder all the way up to the windows on the top floor of the house.

I climb up the ladder. When I reach the nozzle at the top, I aim it at the flames.

WHOOSH!

A powerful stream of water pours from the nozzle.

Soon the flames are gone. The fire is out, and the building is saved.

The family thanks us for saving their home. Then the fire chief sends us back to the fire station.
Good job, firefighters!

Here we are, at Grandma's house at last!
I can't wait to tell her about all the brave things
I would do, if I could drive a fire truck.

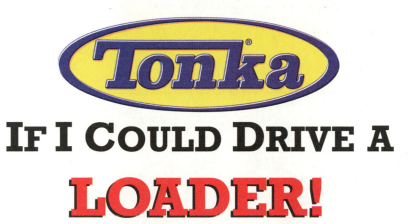

IF I COULD DRIVE A
LOADER!

by Michael Teitelbaum
Illustrated by Uldis Klavins

My name is Ricky, and I love trucks.

I really like playing with my toy trucks and reading books about trucks. That's how I learn all about the ways trucks work.

My favorite truck is the loader.

Today is a special day. I look out the window and see a loader show up, right in front of my house! It's here to dig a ditch for new pipes in the neighborhood.

Wow! Look at that loader pick up big piles of dirt.

What if *I* could drive a loader?

Then I would pour the dirt into a dump truck.

My loader has big wheels. They roll right over rocks and bumpy ground.

Today my neighbors want to plant a new tree in their yard. The tree is much too heavy to move without a big truck. No problem! My loader carries the tree to its new home.

Our town just put in a new baseball field. Now we need a new road to make it easy for people to get there. My loader helps build the road.

First, a truck called a grader makes a smooth path for the new road. Then it's my turn! My loader scoops up the loose dirt and carries it to a dump truck.

Now for the gravel!

At a quarry, my loader shovels gravel into the dump truck. Now the gravel can be spread on the new road. Then the road can be paved.

Next, I use my loader to help a farmer. He needs to prepare a new field to plant his crops.

First, I scrape the grass off the field. I like watching the grass roll into the bucket!

My loader levels the farmer's field. I dig up the high spots and add dirt to the low spots. Finally, the whole field is even. Now the farmer can plow and plant!

In the winter, my loader helps out during a big snowstorm. The plow truck is ready to clear snow from the roads. But it needs salt and sand to spread on the road after it plows. The salt and sand will make the snowy roads less slippery.

There's a big pile of salt and a big pile of sand inside the garage. I fill half of my bucket with salt. Then I'll move to the next pile and scoop up some sand.

With me at the controls, my loader brings the salt and sand out to the plow truck. I dump the mixture into the truck. Then I go back for more.

When the plow truck is full, the driver heads out to plow. After he plows, he'll spread salt and sand on the road.

Uh-oh! The dump truck driver is stuck behind a big pile of snow. He can't get his dump truck out.

But my loader can scoop up and move large mounds of snow! In no time, I dig through the mountain of snow. The dump truck is free!

I would help lots of people, if I could drive a loader.
Maybe someday, I'll get to drive a real one!

IF I COULD DRIVE A

TOW TRUCK!

by Michael Teitelbaum
Illustrated by Jesus Redondo and digitally painted by Steve Mitchell

Uh-oh! One of my cars is broken. No problem, though. I just hook the car up to my tow truck and tow it away!

My tow truck has a powerful engine in the front. I need lots of power to pull heavy cars, trucks, and buses.

In the back of my tow truck I have a winch. A winch is a strong motor attached to a spool of heavy cable.

There is a thick metal hook at the end of the cable. I attach this hook to the cars I tow.

I back my tow truck into position. Then I unwind the cable from the winch. Next, I attach the hook to the front of the broken-down car.

Using the winch's motor, I roll up the cable until it tightens.

As the motor continues to turn the spool, the cable lifts up the front of the car. Now it's ready to be towed.

I get back into the tow truck and tow the car to a repair shop. The driver rides with me in my truck. Soon his car will be back on the road.

My tow truck also helps after accidents. These jobs are called *recoveries*.

This van has flipped over. Luckily, the driver is not hurt. To begin the recovery, I attach the cable to the van.

In another operation, I help recover a small plane that had to make an emergency landing. The plane ended up in a lake, but I'll have it back on dry land in no time!

Once the cable is attached, I drive forward very slowly. Then, using all of its power, my tow truck pulls the plane from the lake. Hooray!